SET A FLAME AJ SAUR

murmuration
press™

Set A Flame
Copyright © 2019 AJ Saur
All rights reserved.

Book design: Amy Cole
Cover art: *Holi*, by sergio34 (detail)

ISBN: 978-1-946671-10-3

Printed in the United States of America

Body text is typeset in Adobe Garamond. Headings are typeset in ABeeZee

Murmuration Press

To contact the publisher concerning this book or others like it, email:
murmurationpress@gmail.com

For today's prophets
and SDG

INTRODUCTION

"In the year that King Uzziah died, I saw the Lord sitting on a throne, high and lofty; and the hem of his robe filled the temple. Seraphs were in attendance above him; each had six wings: with two they covered their faces, and with two they covered their feet, and with two they flew. And one called to another and said: 'Holy, holy, holy is the LORD of hosts; the whole earth is full of his glory.' The pivots on the thresholds shook at the voices of those who called, and the house filled with smoke. And I said: *Woe is me! I am lost, for I am a man of unclean lips, and I live among a people of unclean lips; yet my eyes have seen the King, the LORD of hosts!* Then one of the seraphs flew to me, holding a live coal that had been taken from the altar with a pair of tongs. The seraph touched my mouth with it..." (Isaiah 6:1-7a, NRSV).

REFERENCES

The sixty-six poems in this book arose from my engagement with the sixty-six chapters comprising the Book of the Prophet Isaiah in the Holy Bible. The poems are not reinterpretations of Isaiah's beautiful (and often difficult) words, but rather responses or reflections stimulated by them. The titles of the poems in this collection belong to Isaiah, and references to specific chapters and verses can be found at the back of this book.

ACKNOWLEDGEMENTS

I owe a debt of gratitude to many people for helping me tend the fire of this book. First, to the most amazing poet I know, Jane Wheeler, who made every poem in this book better with her insightful suggestions. Also, my thanks go to Amy Carpenter-Leugs, Nellie deVries, Jerel Domer, and David Witwer who read early drafts of many of these poems and offered helpful improvements. Thanks to Amy Cole of JPL Design Solutions who carried a bright torch with her design of this book.

To my friends Matt Jenson, Keith McAdams, Stephen and Annie Panaggio, and John and Hannah Marie Roberts—thank you for keeping me warm with your love. Your encouragement sustained me through the cold and long nights of Proto-Isaiah (why didn't I choose a shorter book of the Bible?!).

And, finally, to the Prophet Isaiah (however many there are of you), I extend my sincerest gratitude for inviting me into a coal-sized bit of the fire that fueled you. Honestly, it hurt more than I thought it would. Thanks for turning your face upward and showing me what it means to burn *for* someone.

ACCOMPANIMENT

I offer my gratitude to these amazing musicians who crackled in the background as I wrote this collection: Counting Crows, Dana Cunningham, Bob Dylan, Dustin O'Halloran, Over the Rhine, Sleeping at Last, and Bruce Springsteen.

TABLE OF CONTENTS

V

VI

FIRE IS OXIDATION.

~ found poem

I

WHAT ARE YOUR MULTIPLIED SACRIFICES TO ME?

Don't you see
this scarlet trail
is for you to follow?

I pour out
a path
you've not taken.

Why do I suffer
licking dogs, the incessant
buzzing of flies

if not for you?
My body's a banquet. Come
feast at new moon until full

then burn what's left
outside the city walls
or wherever the heavy smoke

will carry, fill your nostrils.
Might I then be inside you
and fearless?

BREATH OF LIFE IS IN THEIR NOSTRILS

Breath bookends our lives.

In between, varying volumes
filled with the intrigues of exhaling—

the panting of young love,
the shallows of heartbreak,

the swell of being seen.
And what of inhaling—

holding another inside
until you must let them go.

We can't build mountains of breath
or stock seas with a stream of them.

We can only give one out at a time,
receive one back.

But we can waste them
blow ourselves off course.

Better to shape breath
into word

harbor it on tongue,
offer it to others.

There is one word
we're all dying to say

our last, first breath.

CAPRICIOUS CHILDREN WILL RULE OVER THEM

Her blind eyes see far beyond
the walls of this nursing home
where she opens her door to you
if you stop some Saturday morning.
She'll take your hand, guide you
with a slow gait to the garden,

tell you the names of the blossoming
flowers by their smell,
introduce you to the shrubs
by the touch of their leaves.
When you share your story,
she will lift it

like a plucked rose to her face,
breathe it in, praise the beauty
of each petal, feel each sharp edge.
She may even describe
what was and is and is to come,
if you listen.

But you need to run.
The kids have soccer practice
and the laundry's piling up.
Perhaps when they're older.
Perhaps when they leave home,
before the grandchildren arrive.

FOR OVER ALL THE GLORY WILL BE A CANOPY

This eggshell ceiling
mantles me
from the striking sun by day,
the reflective reach

of the moon at night.
Over it,
the sky shields
my body

from shooting stars
and spectrum dangers.

Still higher,
the heavens hover
hold planets
in their orbits,

bear mysteries too heavy
for my mass.
But further, in
a space

behind space,
the covered core
burns and burns
speaks in smoke and fire,

a litany of thunder
that cracks overhead.

WHAT MORE WAS THERE TO DO
FOR MY VINEYARD
THAT I HAVE NOT DONE IN IT?

My scattered seed
  has born no fruit
    no sweetness
      on the tongue
        no juice to stain
          the sleeve of a shirt.
The sun, the rain
  the clenched hand
    of the soil could not
      crack its hard shell
        could not tease out
          life's tendrils.
Nothing
  has come out to play
    to dance its fingers
      along a stream
        of so much potential.
          You see what you see
nothing more
  not the core
    that door is bolted.
      The contents
        remain a mystery
          to all
save one
  who tinkers inside—
    so much sweat
      on the brow
        for what?
          Where is the choice vine

the harvest
    hanging heavy
        on the branch
            the flowing wine
                warming the belly?
                    Perhaps even now
the vinedresser is
    buttoning his coat
        shaking so much
            collected dust
                from the tops of
                    his walking shoes.

THERE WILL BE A TENTH PORTION IN IT
LIKE A TEREBINTH WHOSE STUMP REMAINS

During my predawn walk
I stepped over you again
at the place you fell in the path.

I'm surprised no one
has carted you off
to sell to summer campers.

Perhaps others too feel sympathy
for your broken back
for the way your limbs

no longer hold the sky.
Or maybe how you've rested
your head in a patch of lilies

gives us pause.
For we also wish to press
our ears against their petals

to hear how they blossom so white
in this valley of darkness.
Or possibly, we feel sorry

for your stump, jagged
in its grief, without
a cusp of coppiced hope.

As the sun rises,
I turn back to lay
a gentle hand on your base,

to trace your rings
with my finger, following
the paths you've taken,

imagining your reach again
among the clouds.

ASK A SIGN FOR YOURSELF

I have never seen the sun
in reverse, a virgin travail
in childbirth, a fleece drained
of so much dew it pours over
the side of a bowl.

Nor have my eyes beheld
a fish disgorging a prophet
or the bowels of an empty tomb.
But I have witnessed a rainbow
in my backyard, saw it spring

from my sprinkler
one sunny morning. I tried
to hold it, make tangible
the intangible, but it slipped
through.

If only I could have saved
a sliver to carry with me,
a little orange or yellow
in my breast pocket—
not a pot of gold,

just a bit of color
to put in my mouth, to savor
when the sun is hidden,
when the world is gray
and wonderless.

HE SHALL BE YOUR FEAR

Solomon built his temple
in twenty years from cornerstone
to final pillar topped
with pomegranates.

Mine is taking considerably longer
to construct. Each cubit
a measure of quivering,
each quarried stone a shudder.

You may knock
on the decorative doors
of my dread, walk freely
on the ornate floors of my fear,

but what I hope
is your hand
entwined in mine
like lattice—

us
braving this dome
of stars,
the sun.

EACH OF THEM EATS THE FLESH OF HIS OWN ARM

It tastes like chicken
but the tendons tend
to stick in the teeth.

We got hooked
after just a few bites.
Our churches are full

of those who've had their fill.
It's a wonder
there are any arms left

to lift in praise
or elbows to guide
a bride down the aisle.

It's hard to shake
the taste of blood
once you've consumed

the marrow—our legs
don't have a long
future.

But maybe
there's a different meat
to meet our hunger, to satiate

our innate fears, for God
hasn't disappeared, his hand
is still stretched out.

IS THE AXE TO BOAST ITSELF OVER THE ONE WHO CHOPS WITH IT?

We are wood.
But first
we are trees.
We are soil, loose
and turned over.

We are the earth
that spins and spins.
We are the sea
vast and volatile.
Occasionally

we are the staff, held out
parting
waters
producing a dry path
to the Promised Land.

We are not, however
the hand
and never will be
free to grasp, swing, split.
Even Satan is a tool.

FULL OF THE KNOWLEDGE OF THE LORD

Wikipedia works at it—
teams of volunteers
stream data day and night
into a sea of servers
serving courses of material
we consume, but never fill us.

So we order more.
Masticate through
an ever-expanding menu;
mature without matriculating
in a larger body—
one that orders off menu by

falling in at an observatory
to catch a falling star.
One that embraces spaces—
the zeros between the ones—
holes holding the unseen waters
in which we all swim.

THE LORD GOD IS MY SONG

The west winds carry
the scent of a distant sea,
shore up the spirits
of those slaving
in the Assyrian heat.

The smell of salt
revives them, lightens
tongues to move in tune—
from field hand to farm hand
to the framed houses

where lilts lift from the lips
of female servants who grind
coarse meal in the kitchen, heave
under the mass of their masters.
Their songs are not shield or sword

but supple breasts
at which they nurse
a hope, a stream bearing
them to a land swelling
with milk and honey.

II

HYENAS WILL HOWL IN THEIR FORTIFIED TOWERS AND JACKALS IN THEIR LUXURIOUS PALACES

Do you hear it?

The terrible cry
from the temple
trailing you

The bellow
from the bell tower
you can't keep at bay

The roar
from the rampart
resounding around you

Do you hear it?

The wailing
scaling your walls
without waning

The shrieking
continuously shaking
your foundation

The constant
caterwauling
cornering you

Do you hear it?

Stop
running
away

Stop
stopping
your ears

Stop
reaching for
a trigger

Listen.

Something
inside of you
is howling

THE WHOLE EARTH IS AT REST

The wind unwinds, falls
silent lifting not the lightest leaf
to applaud the dawn.

The fire holds
its tongue, reposes
in an ember bed.

The waters calm
sleep under a sheet of glass
gently   spread.

The land creatures land
wonder how long
the world can hold

its breath.

THERE IS NO GREEN THING

Tears stream
collect in pools
of parted

skin—ponds wrinkled
by seventy years
of dry wind

There is no
reflection
of blue sky

or clouds white
in their abundance
Time ripples everything

to black
We try to open
our eyes wider

like greedy hands
grabbing at a dappled
yellow shore

But this too
turns red
A full stop

can't be avoided
or wished away
in paint or song

or even poetry
pushing us uphill
from water's edge

to stand finally
in a field
of clover

YOU WILL MOAN FOR THE RAISIN CAKES OF KIR-HARESETH

It begins
in the belly
of the ship

Not yet a sound
an intonation
on the lips

but a bubble expanding
combining in clusters
of desire

a new molecule
hot and rising
finding cracks

in the deck
of an indifferent
diaphragm

Moving higher
pursues passage on
wind pipe currents

comes to bay
in the throat
From there

sets sail
a human heart
Ripples even

the divine ear

GLEANINGS WILL BE LEFT IN IT
LIKE THE SHAKING OF AN OLIVE TREE

For every tree with an abundance of limbs
there are others more open to the unseen

For every limb bearing a bounty of buds
there are others offering few in the fullness of faith

For every bud producing a flower
there are others forgoing the glory, the gasps

For every flower transfiguring into flesh
there are others that transform a mind for a moment

For every flesh that is reaped
there are others holding firm even when shaken

For every reaping from a calloused hand
there are others deliberate as love

THE BIRDS OF PREY WILL SUMMER ON THEM, THE BEASTS OF THE EARTH WILL WINTER ON THEM

Spring up all you creatures—
raven and wildebeest
bison and boa constrictor—come

from every cold corner
to consume the warm center
claim the dimensions denied you

then we shall be one body
feasting, filling our belly
on praise alone

Sing
sparrow and wolverine
every creepy-crawly thing

Ring out
note after note
starting high

falling
then   rising

BEHOLD, THE LORD IS RIDING ON A SWIFT CLOUD

Does he employ a saddle
throw a leg over
sit tall in the thin air?

Perhaps he prefers bareback—
thighs against white flanks
currents rippling through him?

Others too are astride, flow behind
a wake of wind riders
stealing the world's breath

bowing all things low
like reeds and rushes bent
by a river slow and jealous.

Fishermen hold their nets,
weavers their threads
no line is cast

to catch this thunderhead.

HOW SHALL WE ESCAPE?

I sat at the kiddie table for 25 years
before being lifted by an extra leaf.

How strong my desire to settle there,
to rest in this place of adulthood.

But I couldn't keep pace—
their saying so little

with a wind of many words.
What could I do

but pass the cheesy potatoes,
hand over the bean casserole—

everything circling counterclockwise
until we forget what we're after

like grandma who went to the kitchen
and returned empty-handed?

Perhaps all that matters is the weather,
the score from Sunday's game.

Maybe the borderlands are a territory
from which we cannot return.

WATCHMAN, HOW FAR GONE THE NIGHT?

Do you behold a band of light on the horizon
marching home from war, engaged
no longer with those fingers of darkness
that dig in at the edge of a field,
drag people to a precipice

from which they look but never see?
Dear sentry, don't let us be wombed forever
in black, tortured by a heartbeat—
a sound hidden in sleet, a gray
that won't let day be day. Don't force us

to communicate in code—our voices
in dots and dashes, our words hot
but never touching, then cooling
until they are hard enough to walk on,
to follow without falling through.

Can't you see?
That moving alone and crashing into
are much the same—neither is a dance
we can name like that bright ballet
where he lifts and she rises.

WHAT IS THE MATTER WITH YOU NOW
THAT YOU HAVE GONE UP TO THE HOUSETOP?

Do you need a bit of air, a space
to face the open sky
                    and scream?

A place to lay straight back, stare
into the unblinking eyes
                    of the stars?

Are you trying to escape
that which swarms below
                    all that bites at the heel?

How does it feel when
the rain flows down
                    and everything grows

surrounding you
like an invasive species
                    a climbing vine?

Sure, draw a line, run
in circles, square your shoulders
                    but there's no geometry

that can launch you
from sight, you are
                    the matter

you can't misplace
so eschew the ladder
                    embrace the edge

let yourself fall.

TO DEFILE THE PRIDE OF BEAUTY

What must the sunrise think of itself?
Does it beguile knowingly

trick us into entreating it
with promises we can't keep?

Perhaps it's a ruse of color
that steeps us in awe

sweeps us over the edge
of reason until we're bowing

to a reign of red
the omnipotence of ochre.

Who hasn't been lost
in the green of a pastoral scene,

or marooned by an Old Master?
Who hasn't been led astray

by the gray of a storm cloud
or climbed the heights

of a white-capped mountain?
We're all held captive

by this world at war with gravity.
And when the risen finally falls

we are there to catch it
but that doesn't stop

the breaking.

THE MOON WILL BE ABASHED
AND THE SUN ASHAMED

Do stars dream?
Have nightmares
of celestial bodies naked

before a class of sixth-graders?
Wake screaming, gasping
for air, grasping at cloud covers?

Or do they only daydream,
disappear in broad sunlight
to explore other worlds

where they forever glow above
first kisses, never fail
to receive last-chance wishes,

always guide the lost home?
Maybe they simply envision
a space where antelope, archers,

astronomers don't gaze
at each other from distances
but are jammed together, graced

with the touch of dust upon dust.
There would be no shame then
no need to save face

for everything could shine
more or less
and no one could tell the difference.

A PALACE OF STRANGERS IS A CITY NO MORE

How difficult it must have been
for your mother to summon you
for supper with no name to holler
through the screen door
into the dense heat of summer.

And how could she kiss your cheek
when you have no face
to cup between her warm palms?

No wonder you are the one
who sits at 6th and Madison
with a hat that holds no head.

Even if you could find
your voice down there
dig it out, extend it into air
we have no hands
to receive it.

Ours are in perpetual motion—
moths hungry for light
at the edge of every screen.

Even doors in the suburbs
have dead bolts now
hide mothers who text
10-digit numbers, call
their children forth for dinner

from separate rooms.

THEY COULD ONLY WHISPER A PRAYER

She had been shouting for hours standing
on a bleacher seat in the student section
with banners and bullhorns around her—

a riot of sound bounding onto the field
blocking defenders, surging
for touchdown after touchdown.

The entire town found its voice
rang the bell in the square, honked ecstatically
in the Piggly Wiggly parking lot.

Now the party was pumping
everyone thumping their neighbor
when the players walked in.

She positioned herself atop a chair to watch
the running back advance through the crowd
his hands shiny from a hundred touches.

Her hands were deep in her pockets
but her heart was on her sleeve.
She couldn't call a reverse, leave

the way she came in. Whistles blew within
as people paired up
traveled to the dance floor.

He stood holding a beer
and glanced her way
seemed to mouth a play

in the huddle of himself.

IN THAT DAY A VINEYARD OF WINE, SING OF IT

Jeconiah beget Shealtiel in Babylon
who beget Zerubbabel who beget
Abihud who beget Eliakim. Each son

further from where he started
each a step deeper into a wilderness
that cares not for cultivation,

prefers the feral fathering
of force and demand.
Who can recall a mountaintop

command when blasting through rock,
when taking a lower pass
to the Promised Land?

After all, why lay a plumb line
to harvest perfect light
when one can stick his dynamite anywhere

blow a hole through the beams of heaven.
The valleys now ring with industry,
no one sings a pastoral song.

Who needs a lineage,
a pure note on the tongue,
when he can pay five bucks a bottle

be back next week
for a case?

III

THEY REEL WHILE HAVING VISIONS

We push off from shore
let the oars trail behind
outstretched arms longing

for land. But the strand
doesn't stand still
everything moves

around everything
the way the water
now turns over our blades

propels us toward
the distant horizon.
After a while

we begin to drift, drop
lines, dream of fish—a fixed point
of pride and position.

We envision them latching
our lures, longing to know
the lightness of air

after floating
so long in the dark.
We don't see

the whale off the bow
don't plan a last inhale
find ourselves inside

and sinking.
But there's no bottom here
no tail to hold on to

only the falling
deeper in, while the fins
always churn,

changing the story.

YOUR SPEECH WILL WHISPER FROM THE DUST

I lick my lips
taste dry words
that have crusted
in the corners
everything covered
and nothing seen.

You don't lean in
to listen, instead
move away
to collect samples
from those who mean
what they say.

Lord knows I've tried
to lay a field
of fine phrases—
layers of letters
you could till,
plant in.

But the soil, too thin,
wheeled off down the line
never knew if it was coming
or going. Now I understand
it's the blowing
that makes things brittle

that all you want
is some spittle to fix
on the wind—a thermal
carrying my moisture
leaving dew on
the heavy dirt,

the budding tulip.

THIS IS THE WAY, WALK IN IT

On a gray morning
it's hard to say exactly
how one feels,
so we attempt
to reel our reflection
from a puddle
or a parked car window.

But the light
isn't heavy enough
to reveal the weight
on our shoulders,
the boulders pushed
by angels or demons
having their way.

Perhaps the heft
is our hope,
a rope of gravity
anchoring us in place
as everyone floats
away. Maybe space
is the sin we're all in

that we can't figure out.
Even the sun and stars
have hidden their route,
leaving us to circle.
What can we do
but walk on, accept
the colors that come—

the brown
of a pine cone,
white chalk
on the pavement,
the black hair
of a Border Collie
we ruffle a moment

before she dashes off
toward home.

THE ONE WHO HELPS WILL STUMBLE,
THE ONE WHO IS HELPED WILL FALL

Where were you, love
when you called?

I stood in my stairwell
nonchalant and collected

unaware
of what I would lose.

Apparently,
the sun was shining on you

as you reflected
on feelings remote

as the stars
in their vast array.

Today, I can't recall
if my hands sweated,

if I was headed up
or down

those dimly lit stairs.
Funny how you continue

to cast shadows—
black spaces

tracing my steps.
I remember

the curve of your back
when you lifted me

from the city street
that day I stumbled

over my own feet.
How humbled I was,

though you didn't laugh
or repeat it to friends.

I thought that was love,
but can only conceive

the half of it.

HOW BLESSED YOU WILL BE,
YOU WHO SOW BESIDE ALL WATERS

He doesn't track his toil on a calendar
with thick, black Xs—the buried treasure

of each day. Instead, he banks time
turning soil, burning back the bramble.

The poor become rich
not on a gamble, but when they lay

dead in the dirt. People aren't moved
by money anyway, it's all crash and hurt.

No, we yearn for a net worth,
an unseen undertow that carries us

to a place of yes and go.
It's hard, though, to learn

the art of acceleration—
to trust that up is first down,

begins in the dark and thirst;
that everything flows

from one thing into a ten,
twenty, thirty-fold yield.

The field now a lake
where the deer and oak drink,

where the farmer takes his meal
from the deep.

YOU HAVE CONCEIVED CHAFF

What a lot of trouble this
pushing
      pushing
           pushing
this making space
for another
in an overfull field.

There's no cushioning
to ease our kneeled effort
digging
      digging
           digging
to plant the bulb deep
where it can catch

the undercurrent, sprout, leap
from the top soil—a light
to lead us out of the
churning
      churning
           churning
of sleep, the darkness
of endless motion.

But we chase the wind
a blowing
      blowing
           blowing
we can feel on our skin—
a lotion to soften our lostness?
Who can stand

a lifetime of pregnancy—
that feral glow
growing
      growing
            growing
within
but never coming to term?

THE NIGHT MONSTER WILL SETTLE THERE

She prowls the space
from door frame to bed post,
head raised

as if listening for her name.
She will soon master
this master bedroom.

You stay still
face the wall
and pray for day,

for light's tall beam
to shelter from her
falling shadow.

Nothing

not even a starry lace
edging the window
can alter her gaze

once fixed
on your fledgling attempts
to fly into sleep.

The bedside clock ticks
the minutes she creeps
until she's nigh upon you.

She eats sheep
faster than
you can count them

one by one

she claws over you
filling your mouth with hair—
a final black prayer

in the dead of night.

THE THIRSTY GROUND SPRINGS OF WATER

The sun holds my tongue
until I am as dry and sharp
as a coppered blade of grass.

Now I can cut you,
make you bleed a river
that runs fast and high

but doesn't reach me.
I've never taken tea
in the shade, never lifted

a cup from a saucer,
felt that sensation of sweet
otherness on my lips.

I have pantomimed
the perfect position
of the pinky, the play

of my mouth on the edge
of that possibility.
But how do I drink?

How hollow is thinking,
I can't conceive
your stream,

nor play the deer
and dip myself in.
No, I fear this flow

is a mirage of sand
where I'll eat land after land
and gain no ground.

Will you have me found
dining on dirt
when your dam lets loose?

THEY ANSWERED NOT A WORD

If you had heard
the cloistered sisters
sit down to table
you would not
have heard much,

less cackle and cluck,
more the sound
of a noon bell struck
and the reverberations
of air grasped in hands

folded for prayer.
Then, if you were lucky,
the chime of metal spoon
against metal bowl,
the soul stirred

through the plain chant
of corn chowder. Then, torn
bread like a rent spirit,
a head bent low
to save each crumb.

How slow
the movements,
how unceremonious the lifting
of the ceramic cup to lips,
the slide

of water
wholly absent of splash
or the dash
to get on with things.
For there is nothing

to press on to,
no string of words
to plant,
no heavy paragraph
to buttress.

Only a fallow tongue
occasionally tussled
by a breeze of laughter
blowing through.
New revelations

not in noun or verb
but in slant looks,
books of touch on skin,
a voluminous chin
worn with tears.

WILL [I] BE SPARED?

I don't know how
to fluff the pillow
the way you like it.

The necessary care
for fullness,
for down

that lifts up,
so gently holds
your every thought.

How unfair
its ease in molding
to your face, your hair

while I still trace you
on the walls
of my mind.

Will I ever find
enough spaces
to pool your tears,

to let my fabric
absorb your hurt?
I can weave my way

to your lips
for a bedtime kiss,
but can't compete

with Egyptian cotton,
with a night
of perfect cushioning.

I only ask
that occasionally
you'd lay

your head
on my chest
let me bear you

through the dark,
carry you
on the soft tide

of my heartbeat.

FROM DAY UNTIL NIGHT
YOU MAKE AN END OF ME

Eyes watch

as you send the scorching sun—
an army besieging a city.

There is nowhere it isn't pressing in.
Dawn's become sin, a damn shame.

Everything's now aflame with your touch.
The sand, the pavement, the car door handle

all hold your anger. Shadows
have become strangers.

Shade offers no retreat
from the heat of your breath.

Hour by long hour our sloughs are slain,
drawn into the annals of hot air.

Not soon enough, dusk
greets our sorry stains—

the ones you step over
on your way to wherever you're going.

And how long can those stay?
When you send in your city-sweeper

will that reaper cleanse all?
Raze everything up,

even I?

HE SHOWED THEM ALL HIS TREASURE HOUSE

One can measure
the space
between   us

in cubits
of stacked
silence

each minute
a gold bar put away
for a day that won't come.

Some still hold hope
in bronze ages—a pay
they can weigh in years,

unfold like crisp centuries
to lay
in your palm.

But I am seconds
from where I want to be,
free to give all as alms,

to see
my dazzling return
to homelessness.

Keep your muted millennia
in marble houses
for all I care

but don't treat me
to a tour.
I'm content

out in the cold
with nothing
but the note

in my throat,
a silvered psalm
for the naked,

for those who tell time
in touch, offer coins
as a caress

that can tip
my scale.

IV

ALL FLESH IS GRASS

Yes,
the highest hill
could sprout
your next of kin

but most of us
are spread thin
on the outskirts
of some forlorn place

like Fargo or Galveston.
What does it look like
to win when there's
drought after drought,

when the merciless sun
demands salutation?
How many of us
have yellowed

burn like the prophet Jonah
who cursed the worm
for eating through
his unearned shade?

It hurts the neck
to look heavenward,
our blades resist
the sharpening wind but

bend
for summer showers,
worship
the downpour.

Had we hands,
we'd constantly knock
at the door of the one
who unspools   the world,

knits the cool of night.
But we're stuck in soil,
can't shake it loose—
this earth that takes

and takes, breaks
us down
until we're pushing   up
another generation,

praying they'll kiss
the feet
of the clouds, taste
that blue sweetness.

COASTLANDS, LISTEN TO ME IN SILENCE

I am on the edge
of a tsunami of sound.
I will hearken
to your pounding

on my shore
with sealed lips,
a cove
of perfect quiet.

Such a chore it'll be
to collect the debris
from your discourse,
drift wood

fixed in a heavy sand
of shoulds and oughts.
But I can be taught
to stack cords

without singing aloud,
without turning the key
to free the proud tongue.
That'd be easy, I thought,

until reality brought
your call in a bottle.
Give me wind,
the palm trees

bent
at your arrival,
the full throttle sea
slamming into me.

IT SET HIM AFLAME

How tame it seems now,
how unprofound, the mixing
of spirits in a glass, the sound
of cubes swirled before the sip,
the swallow.

Did it burn your chest,
did your lips smolder? Let me see
the smoke in your eyes,
turn your hand over and I'll follow
your life line like a fuse.

I explode
while you exist
so self-contained.
How much fire can you hold
in your frame?

I tire of sweating, of living
eternally in your light.
I can't handle
the ember
you left behind.

But I can pour myself
a scotch, a tumbler of heat—
just enough to scorch
my memory, not so much
to reignite the heart.

I ACT AND WHO CAN REVERSE IT?

Here's a fact:

the white-tailed deer can travel
at 30 miles per hour—

a tad slower than the speed
of my hand to my heart

when a doe powers past
the wooded path where I stand.

Her silent glide
into a glade

makes me wonder
what I did wrong.

Who can understand
this dash to depart

like the flash
of the goldfinch

flying off
or the splash

of the pickerel frog
when I arrive

at pond's edge?
Must we always spread

to survive? I felt
most alive when you laid

your head
on my shoulder,

bound your arm in mine
as we walked together

to the scenic outlook.
There's seemingly no end

of new books on the Big Bang,
you said as we neared the ledge,

each loudly acclaiming
the delight of scattershot.

We saw no creatures
at the summit when you

pulled away
to film a video on your phone.

How often do you rewind
those clouds

to that moment
before they drift, break

apart?

IS THERE NOT A LIE IN MY RIGHT HAND?

I tie tight to this page every word
with a bond of black ink. Don't think
of the caged bird singing, rather
a hammer ringing as each railroad spike
is driven in, then language like a lady
roped to the tracks and screaming.

Surely there's more hope than that,
you'll say, what of the azure sky
after a midday storm, or the way
a man embraces a woman like an opened
coat? What of the moon, you may note,
or the dog at our side?

Yes, I could compose some quote-worthy quip,
stress a tenet of sacred belief, even undress
to bare my own shriveled flesh. But can you harness
these words, ride them like a winged horse
to heaven? How honest is this hand that leads you,
brings you now to a field of white

with nothing left to offer?

YOU ARE A GOD WHO HIDES HIMSELF

What manner of stealth are the stars
spied on this cloudless night?

What white lie are the lilacs
sniffed out by every lifted nose?

What supposed silence
is this sparrow's evening song?

How wrong
every sense must be

or insane, or stretched taut by time
and made lame.

Sever the tie then,
shatter the frame, free us

to know nonsense
as the sixth sense

which we might call love
or claim in death

or discover as that space
where everything is

and nothing is not.

I WILL BEAR YOU

Carrying your heavy volumes up
the stairs nearly broke my back

in two, but I didn't share
that weight. Instead,

I fed on your words
as we unboxed the kitchen,

could relate to your mom
those last weeks of gestation

awaiting a breach, a break
from the heaviness of breath.

Where on earth can one go
to spread mass

be delivered from gravity,
free to levitate

like the swallowtail butterfly
that lifts lushness in silence,

pollinates another's pleasure
without a sigh?

STAND FAST IN YOUR SPELLS

You cast it over me like a net
catch me by the tale
of some foreign land
where women still lift skirts

to press grapes with feet
feel skins between skin
like the sand and dirt
my toes once knew in childhood.

You stress each beat of the story
with the baton of your hand
and my imagination plays along
with that band of red ants

madly drinking drops
of dripped juice.
And when you say your stop
is next, I grow sad,

for you've hypnotized me
with the sweep of their arms
heaving bucket after bucket
of pulp—a train of such sweetness

I would follow it to any end.
And when an abrupt bend
in the tracks forces you back
to your seat, a hope

arises within me like the lifting
of jugs upon their heads
that instead you'll stay
and say more about the wooden floor

where they dance,
where everyone becomes intoxicated
by a swirl brighter
than the brightest burgundy.

YOUR FOREHEAD BRONZE

My breath led
to condensation—
two   scores
of steam marking the way
like dogsled tracks
through the snow.

Mush, Mush, I said
urging my team forward
but no surge
could scratch the surface,
could allay my fear
of disappearing.

I tried to steal a kiss
before your lips hardened,
before your alloy
became aloof
and preoccupied
with patina.

Yet, I still see the light
in your eyes,
can't help
letting you in. Love
is no mere reflection,
and night's more than

a sighing
at the connection
of copper and tin.
The soft animal within you
can yet twin with air,
can harness a flow home

to warm before a fire, feel
the cabin creak and sway
with the wind.

V

———

THEIR PASTURE WILL BE ON ALL BARE HEIGHTS

Everywhere's a stair
     and someone
         just took a step.

You don't need to dream
     to discover
         angels ascending

and descending
     only let the hard seed
         of your heart open

to the unseen
     air that streams around you.
         But beware, you'll go

where you don't want to,
     flow to a foreign land
         where to know is to see.

There, trees in the field
     bear continual fruit
         and no one lifts a ladder.

Yet, the hand can handle
     only so much,
         and the soul even

less.
     Best begin slow, grazing
         the flesh with finger,

witnessing wonder
      rise up to meet you. Though,
            the greeting's only natural

and no special show
      of feeling. Still,
            you'll reel

until you find
      above
            below.

To come
      is to go,
            and all

moves together
      on a breeze
            like a meadow

of wild flowers.

THE MOTH WILL EAT THEM

I'm not as well-fitted
as your cashmere sweater.
I fray at the neck,

leave your skin cold.
My gold fringe
has lost its luster,

can't muster that color
which so captivated you.
No longer close-knit, I stick out

in places you avoid
for fear of snagging a thread
you can't outrun.

Yes, dear me
better to leave things
unsaid and tucked into

that trunk at the foot
of your bed. But, maybe
dead isn't dead

as you suppose.
For even there,
in your chest, grows

an opening
in the darkness, a white
flutter of wing beat—

each tip touching, touching
your hiddenness
creating a heat

hotter than wool,
a light unraveling
the blackest of nights.

ROUSE YOURSELF

Most beasts need the bark of a dog,
the hark of some angelic host
to speed them toward the sea.

      Me?

Drum up a dragon to seed a course
through the night or, better still,
might I stay here on my knees,

      lay low for eternity?

After all, there's no freedom
without a say. But hey (soft laugh),
your teeth look tall and your claws sharp.

      Shall we call this a draw,

agree to play apart?
True, you had me at the start,
but that was long ago

      before I knew all I now know.

Wait, wait, go slow
my eyes are bigger than my heart,
can't quickly adjust to light.

      Yes, 10 plagues seems about right,

but why does my chest
still feel so tight? Perhaps
it's the 600,000 sheep in flight

with a single staff holding sway.

I may be daft,
but are you sure
this is the way?

MARRED MORE THAN ANY MAN

Just one slow car in the left lane
can make plain the stalled state
of a soul. After all,

who can spot a stain
when traveling at light speed?
Of course, at any rate,

our self-advancing refrain
may dull the brain to death—
that dead-end or detour

or destiny. But does anyone get
a free pass to paradise?
Sure, that'd be nice

like a leisurely drive
along the Aegean Sea
but reality brings a strong rain

when the top's down.
We're all drowning
in our own devices

with too few finding
a drain. Even Bob Dylan
missed his train, is stuck

in Mobile
with the masses—
wet and blue.

Yes, one can bet
on the jack of hearts,
hold true to the ace

in the hole,
yet it may be a lack
that leads the way—

souls on empty
that carry us through
to that far-off future

today.

A SHEEP BEFORE ITS SHEARERS

How certain the trees are in spring,
their revelry of leaves unfurled

for us to see. Don't they recall
the fall, the sheer loss of everything

save life and limb?
How do they stand

tall when naked, toss
their fate to winter winds?

Scripture says
Take up your cross

but that's hogwash, a lie
if we only call the downtrodden

to die. True, a sigh is a sigh
no matter who utters it, yet

some hearts can't slip the stitch
as turn after turn passes by.

A bleat's only one type of cry,
another burns without heat

like an endless supply of dry ice.
Yes, some can rely on a sweater

but what warms best may be
a body resting in summer pasture,

a soft breeze spooling off
the willows nearby.

LIKE THE DAYS OF NOAH

before we raised towers to the sky,
before we flew into them

with the hope of attaining heaven,
power came down from on high

lifting us up like leavened bread.
Every cup ran over

until there was nothing left
to tie one on to.

All but a few drifted,
no match for a rent firmament.

Why do our soundings
now make no sound?

What happened to that damn
pounding producing a dry land

where pair after pair now stand?
Okay then, take us

by the hand, but don't leave us
without a stair, a way to tail you—

if we simply follow,
tread drop after drop,

will we stream
ahead of the arc, embark

without stopping?

WHY SPEND MONEY FOR WHAT IS NOT BREAD?

It is written to cast it
upon water
then stand fast

awaiting its return.
But what's the fate
of the hooked worm

suspended between above
and that deep below?
Is it a sort of sleep

where everything moves
in slow motion
to some intended end

we can't know? And, still
I won't let go of love
or the notion of fullness

like the extended belly
of Jonah's great fish.
So, I fillet my days, anticipate

the overflow.
But believing in a brimming basket
is wishful at best, forgets

the black clouds swimming
across sky, sowing
their seed until I suffocate.

Our forbearers too cried out
for meat, pleaded for a break from manna.
A word spread, though,

unsettles and irritates
until we sink
into it,

feel
our bodies rise
with the weight.

VI

TOMORROW WILL BE LIKE TODAY, ONLY MORE SO

Spending every second below deck
slows time at first then suspends
direction until all one knows
is the surrounding sea—

a ceaseless entity some call
nirvana, or *freedom* more generally.
Others, though, would sooner sink
than float in this heavenly stasis.

See, they want to flow
travel like a breeze ascending
then falling low. They praise
the thermal that goes and goes,

the pelican that shows the way
to glory. But sin entered in,
pitch-poled every story. Now
each beginning's an end,

each end terminally so.
No, wait, one can tack this trend, bend
history as every keeled life catches
wind, every day's a heeling.

INFLAME YOURSELVES AMONG THE OAKS

At the stroke of midnight
the sun is so low
the moon reflects only
a sliver
of its shame.

The rest goes unclaimed
lost forever in that space
between wall
and bed frame. Even there,
every dropped

name costs a career,
every fall
is said to be endless.
Perhaps that's the price of fame—
all heads extend to see

the descent.
But those who look twice
discover a bend
in their own tree, a history
sown by a thousand fire starters.

Yet, we never tire of tending
someone else's tinder,
retreating into the smoke
of their infamy.
Better, it seems to us,

to stand free
a strand untouched
by such an inferno.

Though,
a solo show
shows little vibrancy
compared to a vast grove aglow
at sunrise.

GIVE YOURSELF TO THE HUNGRY

I'm no top-shelf delight.
You'll have to fight through

calloused skin to get in.
Even then, the tendons

may win, choke you to death.
Sure, a bite might offer

some juicy insight,
treat you to a succulent memory

like the time I stayed up all night
to keep the moon company.

But soon, you'll wonder
how my Fulbright scholarship essay

and a week-long road trip to the Rockies
left you empty.

Even as you lick Paddington Bear
off the wallpaper

of my childhood bedroom,
you'll only care what's next

to consume—
my sixth-grade permed hair

or that sperm whale looming large
off the stern

of our pleasure cruise
then, in a second,

gone.

FROM THAT WHICH IS CRUSHED

Sixteen-hundred pounds of pressure
will pulverize the human pelvis—
the sound of which surprises
the ear, slithering in silently
then a biting pitch when bone
gives way.

Fear too lies
in wait for that moment
when everything seems okay. Emerging
from the overgrown thicket
of the mind to poison
a perfectly decent day.

Had I known what rises up
and rattles, would I have tread
a different path? But how can I
battle a body that betrays?
Who's to say when it will uncoil,
strike at heel or heart or head?

It's played me from the start,
knows the notes to make me
plead, yowl, pray aloud.
How will I escape the scraping
of pestle on mortar, the shedding
of all my skin?

When I'm fully in a vise-grip,
my sins counted like colored bands,
will you squeeze the handle
until I dissipate
into strands of shimmering snakelets—
a charm for every occasion?

WHO ARE THESE WHO FLY LIKE DOVES TO THEIR LATTICES?

The saddest I've ever been
was when they chopped down
the box elder planted
on the day of my birth.
In various spots it stopped

producing, had a pox leaving
a patchwork of vegetation—
branches bare here and there.
But the earth held it tight,
got carried away

fighting with the tree removal men.
When I returned after work, saw
the sawdust, surveyed the large hole,
my soul fluttered with memories
seeing a younger me free

from responsibility, climbing
in summer, nestling in limbs,
listening for the caw
of blue jays just above.
Then that spring when I first fell

in love, sunk my knife in
to carve crude letters
with a shaky heart
surrounding them. Even after
the fledgling part of me left town

starving for something better,
I could never fill it like I do now
laying shovelful after shovelful
of dirt where roots used to be.
In time, grass will grow

and no one will know the beautiful
life that played here in the wind,
stayed true to every bird
that flew off
and came back again.

RAISE UP THE FORMER DEVASTATIONS

When you ask for a pass
on the cup, whose hand
do you imagine
will last hold it, lifting it
like an entire vineyard
to the lips?

Yes, we could take sip
after sip, swallow a small crop
of faithfulness. But who
might untread the nations,
reverse the pulping of
a thousand generations?

Steady were the fingers
that first sculpted the clay,
formed the trunk, the head,
the leaf opening
to daylight. Everything lived,
grew to full height,

was loaded to bear
with clusters of sweetest fruit.
All care was given
but the root sought wonders
underground, found a stairway
down, leading to places

where people lay low
so no one has to fall.
There they can only
recall the first floor,
that open door to dirt
where to live is to crawl.

What is tall anyway?
Who could stand it
if it meant downing
gallons of gall, building
sky-rises out of so much
wormwood?

YOU WILL BE CALLED BY A NEW NAME

But not yet.

For now, you'll remain
Ryan or Ruth
Jerry or Jane
or (God forbid)
Skylar, Rain, or River.

Nature will exclaim nothing
different than your dad
when he heralds you for dinner
or when an ex-flame takes it in vain—
leaves it hanging

in the branches like a limp
balloon.
Life will linger
day
upon day

until maybe you're carved
in the trunk of a tree,
tattooed on a lover's limb,
or tagged and retagged
like so much graffiti.

A handful will go
undercover,
select a new identity. But no one
can break free from a story started.
It must continue

until you're in front of
your bathroom mirror peering
into someone's eyes,
materialized
as the moniker you are—

no sage or star or saint,
no sinner or savior or soothsayer,
just a word,
a single layer no deeper than
your appellation when first planted

on paper. You
can air your designation
while standing in the shower,
even sing it slow and stark,
but the echo is the shadow part.

To know the whole
you have to lay down
all position and power,
then it'll ring out like a bell
on Easter morn, an endless

chiming.

I HAVE TRODDEN THE WINE TROUGH ALONE

Standing in a line of one
there's no soul before or behind,
no family of four trying to press
into a space that's all mine.

Even the sun knows
not to shine, keeps hidden
below the horizon.
So the dark sees to the vines,

assures that not a single grape escapes.
Time marks no pace here,
wipes its hands of every new year,
every hope of holding.

What's left is the liminal crush
between love and loathing, the molding
of feet into pestle or patented machine
that pounds and mashes

until each tread's a pulverized prayer,
each step sounds of fear.
If there's anyone left,
should anyone care,

I'm now headed for home
to draw a bath,
to sip from a stemless glass
as the water turns red.

WHEN YOU DID AWESOME THINGS WE DID NOT EXPECT

The loon on the lake
sang my secret name
calling me waterside to see
tall spruce bow at first light
—lay their heads low—

hear wind whisper in waves,
worship the unseen flow
that moves the world.
But I'm a skipped stone.
Small

splashes
living in abbreviated
dashes   of loving
and letting
go.

Why is the heart so slow to turn
on another's axis?
Why does every dip
feel like death
instead of practice?

The blue heron has now arrived,
gliding in on grace, receives
the ripples as a quiet gift.
But I squawk at each trip north,
each cycle that hides

the end.
I've been here before
and don't want to come this way again.
Summoned to this shore,
I stand on the edge of what

I don't know.
When suddenly
a narrow ray bends me
in two
and I find someone

holding my hand, not letting go.

AN HEIR OF MY MOUNTAINS

His hair has thinned
like the air
like the trees
sparse
and leaning into headwinds.

He makes his bed of tundra,
of that which cradles dreams loosely—
not for lack of care
or a thick dread
but because they must release

seed a stair for climbing.
But we can't bear
the thought of lifting knee
to some heavy unseen
height when right in front,

or slightly below,
there's an abundance
of slim beauties to grasp.
Yet, time hugs nothing tight
lets everything go

beyond the holding.
Still, clocks
have little foresight for the bold
whose open hands offer
no fight as blow after blow

shifts the soul
carries past cave and clouds
to fully exposed cliff,
bared to sun, a birthright
in radiant gold.

FIRE WILL NOT BE QUENCHED

I sought to retire
to the wingback chair
to hover by the window

in the lengthening shadows
as the sun tucked in
for the night.

But I struck my toe
on the side table, lit it
like a match burning brief

and bright. Apparently,
there's no place to hide from oneself,
to fit the soul

into some dark corner of space
where flesh doesn't launch
flare after flare

to light up the brain.
Damn the efficiency of pain,
such an able fuse for faith.

You met Moses
in a shimmering shrub,
Peter in a rooster comb,

but with me
you come as lightning,
set in my lips a flame.

Now, every verb's electricity
every noun hangs in air—
a sear

all can hear,
a talon grabbing at heart,
carrying to mountaintop

where each sharp
stop
is the start

to the next blazing line
in the story.

REFERENCES

All titles in this collection are from the Book of the Prophet Isaiah in the Holy Bible.

Scripture references as detailed below (excepting Isaiah 18:6) taken from:

The NEW AMERICAN STANDARD BIBLE®
Copyright © 1960, 1962, 1963, 1968, 1971, 1972,
1973, 1975, 1977, 1995
by The Lockman Foundation. Used by permission.

Scripture reference for Isaiah 18:6 taken from:

The Holy Bible, English Standard Version,
Copyright © 2001 by Crossway Bibles,
a division of Good News Publishers. Used by permission.
All rights reserved.

• • •

1:11 "'**What are you multiplied sacrifices to Me?**' says the LORD. 'I have had enough of burnt offerings of rams and the fat of fed cattle; and I take no pleasure in the blood of bulls, lambs or goats.'"

2:22 "Stop regarding man, whose **breath of life is in his nostrils;** for why should he be esteemed?"

3:4 "And I will make mere lads their princes, and **capricious children will rule over them.**"

4:5   "Then the LORD will create over the whole area of Mount Zion and over her assemblies a cloud by day, even smoke, and the brightness of a flaming fire by night; **for over all the glory will be a canopy.**"

5:4   "**'What more was there to do for My vineyard that I have not done in it?** Why, when I expected it to produce good grapes did it produce worthless ones?'"

6:13   "'Yet **there will be a tenth portion in it,** and it will again be subject to burning, **like a terebinth** or an oak **whose stump remains** when it is felled. The holy seed is its stump.'"

7:11   "'**Ask a sign for yourself** from the LORD your God; make it deep as Sheol or high as heaven.'"

8:13   "'It is the LORD of hosts whom you should regard as holy. And **He shall be your fear**, and He shall be your dread.'"

9:20   "They slice off what is on the right hand but still are hungry, and they eat what is on the left hand but they are not satisfied; **each of them eats the flesh of his own arm.**"

10:15   "**Is the axe to boast itself over the one who chops with it?** Is the saw to exalt itself over the one who wields it? That would be like a club wielding those who lift it, or like a rod lifting him who is not wood."

11:9   "They will not hurt or destroy in all My holy mountain, for the earth will be **full of the knowledge of the LORD** as the waters cover the sea."

12:2   "'Behold, God is my salvation, I will trust and not be afraid; for **the LORD God is my** strength and **song**, and He has become my salvation.'"

13:22   **"Hyenas will howl in their fortified towers and jackals in their luxurious palaces.** Her fateful time also will soon come and her days will not be prolonged."

14:7   "'**The whole earth is at rest** and is quiet; they break forth into shouts of joy.'"

15:6   "For the waters of Nimrim are desolate. Surely the grass is withered, the tender grass died out, **there is no green thing.**"

16:7   "Therefore Moab will wail; everyone of Moab will wail. **You will moan for the raisin cakes of Kir-hareseth** as those who are utterly stricken."

17:6   "Yet **gleanings will be left in it like the shaking of an olive tree,** two or three olives on the topmost bough, four or five on the branches of a fruitful tree, declares the LORD, the God of Israel."

18:6   "They shall all of them be left to the birds of prey of the mountains and to the beasts of the earth. And **the birds of prey will summer on them,** and all **the beasts of the earth will winter on them.**"

19:1   "The oracle concerning Egypt. **Behold, the LORD is riding on a swift cloud** and is about to come to Egypt; the idols of Egypt will tremble at His presence, and the heart of the Egyptians will melt within them."

20:6   "So the inhabitants of this coastland will say in that day, 'Behold, such is our hope, where we fled for help to be delivered from the king of Assyria; and we, **how shall we escape?**'"

21:11   "The oracle concerning Edom. One keeps calling to me from Seir, '**Watchman, how far gone is the night?** Watchman, how far gone is the night?'"

22:1   "The oracle concerning the valley of vision. **What is the matter with you now, that you have** all **gone up to the housetop**s?"

23:9   "The LORD of hosts has planned it, **to defile the pride of** all **beauty**, to despise all the honored of the earth."

24:23   "Then **the moon will be abashed and the sun ashamed**, for the LORD of hosts will reign on Mount Zion and in Jerusalem, and His glory will be before His elders."

25:2   "For You have made a city into a heap, a fortified city into a ruin; **a palace of strangers is a city no more**, it will never be rebuilt."

26:16   "O LORD, they sought You in distress; **they could only whisper a prayer**, your chastening was upon them."

27:2   **"In that day, 'a vineyard of wine, sing of it!'"**

28:7   "And these also reel with wine and stagger from strong drink: the priest and the prophet reel with strong drink, they are confused by wine, they stagger from strong drink; **they reel while having visions**, they totter when rendering judgment."

29:4   "Then you will be brought low; from the earth you will speak, and from the dust where you are prostrate your words will come. Your voice will also be like that of a spirit from the ground, and **your speech will whisper from the dust**."

30:21   "Your ears will hear a word behind you, '**This is the way, walk in it**,' whenever you turn to the right or to the left."

31:3   "Now the Egyptians are men and not God, and their horses are flesh and not spirit; so the LORD will stretch out His hand, and **he who helps will stumble and he who is helped will fall**, and all of them will come to an end together."

32:20   "**How blessed will you be, you who sow beside all waters**, who let out freely the ox and the donkey."

33:11   "'**You have conceived chaff**, you will give birth to stubble; My breath will consume you like fire.'"

34:14   "The desert creatures will meet with the wolves, the hairy goat also will cry to its kind; yes, **the night monster will settle there** and will find herself a resting place."

35:7   "The scorched land will become a pool and **the thirsty ground springs of water**; in the haunt of jackals, its resting place, grass becomes reeds and rushes."

36:21   "But **they** were silent and **answered** him **not a word**; for the king's commandment was, 'Do not answer him.'"

37:11   "Behold, you have heard what the kings of Assyria have done to all the lands, destroying them completely. So **will you be spared?**"

38:12   "'Like a shepherd's tent my dwelling is pulled up and removed from me; as a weaver I rolled up my life. He cuts me off from the loom; **from day until night You make an end of me.**'"

39:2   "Hezekiah was pleased, and **showed them all his treasure house**, the silver and the gold and the spices and the precious oil and his whole armory and all that was found in his treasuries. There was nothing in his house nor in all his dominion that Hezekiah did not show them."

40:6   "A voice says, 'Cry out.' Then he answered, 'What shall I cry out?' **All flesh is grass**, and all its loveliness is like the flower of the field."

41:1   "'**Coastlands, listen to Me in silence**, and let the peoples gain new strength; let them come forward, then let them speak; let us come together for judgment.'"

42:25   "So He poured out on him the heat of His anger and the fierceness of battle; and **it set him aflame** all around, yet he did not recognize it; and it burned him, but he paid no attention."

43:13   "'Even from eternity I am He, and there is none who can deliver out of My hand; **I act and who can reverse it?**'"

44:20   "He feeds on ashes; a deceived heart has turned him aside. And he cannot deliver himself, nor say, '**Is there not a lie in my right hand?**'"

45:15   "Truly, **You are a God who hides Himself**, O God of Israel, Savior!"

46:4   "'Even to your old age I will be the same, and even to your graying years **I will bear you**! I have done it, and I will carry you; and I will bear you and I will deliver you.'"

47:12   "'**Stand fast** now **in your spells** and in your many sorceries with which you have labored from your youth; perhaps you will be able to profit, perhaps you may cause trembling.'"

48:4   "'Because I know that you are obstinate, and your neck is an iron sinew and **your forehead bronze**,...'"

49:9   "'Saying to those who are bound, "Go forth," to those who are in darkness, "Show yourselves." Along the roads they will feed, and **their pasture will be on all bare heights**.'"

50:9   "Behold, the Lord God helps Me; who is he who condemns Me? Behold, they will all wear out like a garment; **the moth will eat them**."

51:17   "**Rouse yourself!** Rouse yourself! Arise, O Jerusalem, you who have drunk from the Lord's hand the cup of His anger; the chalice of reeling you have drained to the dregs."

52:14   "Just as many were astonished at you, My people, so His appearance was **marred more than any man** and His form more than the sons of men."

53:7   "He was oppressed and He was afflicted, yet He did not open His mouth; like a lamb that is led to slaughter, and like **a sheep** that is silent **before its shearers**, so He did not open His mouth."

54:9   "'For this is **like the days of Noah** to Me, when I swore that the waters of Noah would not flood the earth again; so I have sworn that I will not be angry with you nor will I rebuke you.'"

55:2   "'**Why** do you **spend money for what is not bread**, and your wages for what does not satisfy? Listen carefully to Me, and eat what is good, and delight yourself in abundance.'"

56:12   "'Come,' they say, 'let us get wine, and let us drink heavily of strong drink; and **tomorrow will be like today, only more so.**'"

57:5   "'...who **inflame yourselves among the oaks**, under every luxuriant tree, who slaughter the children in the ravines, under the clefts of the crags?'"

58:10   "'And if you **give yourself to the hungry** and satisfy the desire of the afflicted, then your light will rise in darkness and your gloom will become like midday.'"

59:5   "They hatch adders' eggs and weave the spider's web; he who eats of their eggs dies, and **from that which is crushed** a snake breaks forth."

60:8   "'**Who are these who fly like** a cloud and like the **doves to their lattices?**'"

61:4   "Then they will rebuild the ancient ruins, they will **raise up the former devastations**; and they will repair the ruined cities, the desolations of many generations."

62:2   "The nations will see your righteousness, and all kings your glory; and **you will be called by a new name** which the mouth of the LORD will designate."

63:3   "'**I have trodden the wine trough alone**, and from the peoples there was no man with Me. I also trod them in My anger and trampled them in My wrath; and their lifeblood is sprinkled on My garments, and I stained all My raiment.'"

64:3   "**When You did awesome things** which **we did not expect**, You came down, the mountains quaked at Your presence."

65:9   "'I will bring forth offspring from Jacob, and **an heir of My mountains** from Judah; even My chosen ones shall inherit it, and My servants will dwell there.'"

66:24   "'Then they will go forth and look on the corpses of the men who have transgressed against Me. For their worm will not die and their **fire will not be quenched**; and they will be an abhorrence to all mankind.'"

www.ingramcontent.com/pod-product-compliance
Lightning Source LLC
La Vergne TN
LVHW041157080426
835511LV00006B/635